I CAN BE A

CARPENTER

By Dee Lillegard

Prepared under the direction of Robert Hillerich, Ph.D.

In memory of Donald Winfred Lillegard, Master Carpenter

 CHILDRENS PRESS ®

CHICAGO

Library of Congress Cataloging-in-Publication Data
Lillegard, Dee.
   I can be a carpenter.
   (I can be)
   Includes index.
   Summary: Examines different kinds of jobs in the
field of carpentry and highlights the necessary education
and training.
   1. Carpenters—Juvenile literature. 2. Carpentry—
Junvenile literature. [1. Carpentry—Vocational guidance.
2. Vocational guidance. 3. Occupations] I. Title.
II. Series: I can be.
TH5604.L47   1986   694'.023   86-9676
ISBN 0-516-01884-1

PICTURE DICTIONARY

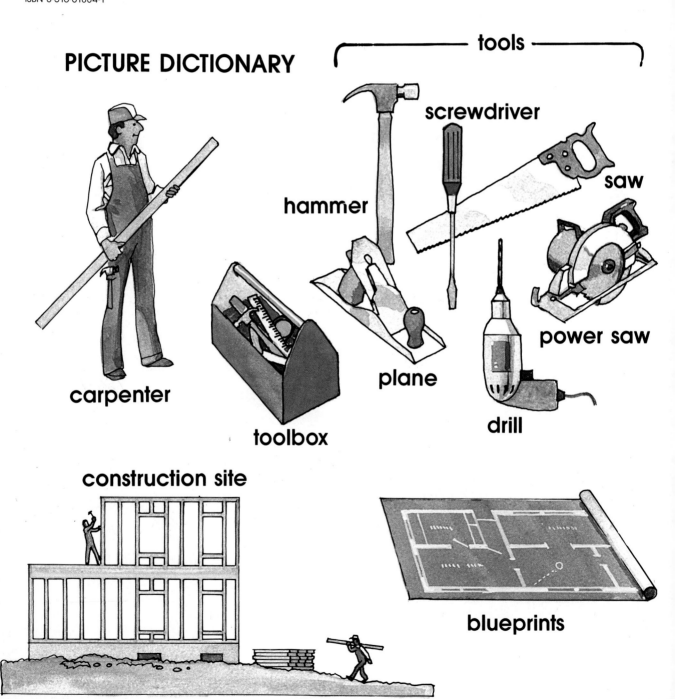

tools

carpenter

toolbox

hammer

screwdriver

saw

plane

power saw

drill

construction site

blueprints

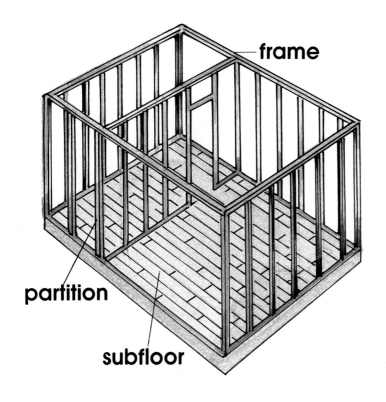

frame

partition

subfloor

window frame

cabinet

set

TV studio

scaffold

Hammers are tapping. Power saws are buzzing. There's a fresh, clean smell of wood in the air. Carpenters are at work!

Have you ever been to a construction site? Have you ever watched carpenters building a house or a shopping center? A carpenter's job is *noisy*.

carpenter

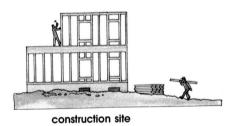
construction site

power saw

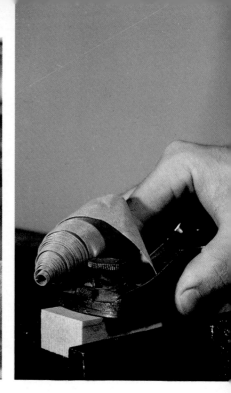

Left: Many carpenters use a handy tool pouch that hangs from the belt.
Center: Using a hammer to nail two boards together. Right: A plane
shaves off the surface of a board to make it smooth.

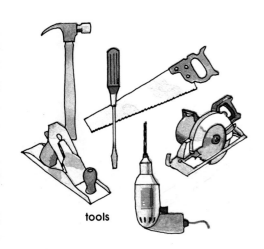

tools

Carpenters work with wood. They use many kinds of tools to build things that last. A good carpenter selects the very best tools and takes good care of them.

6

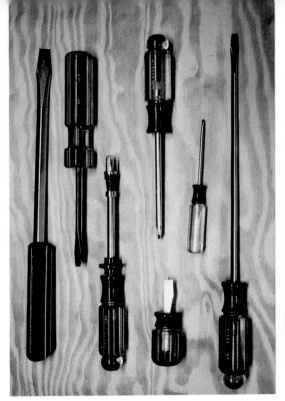

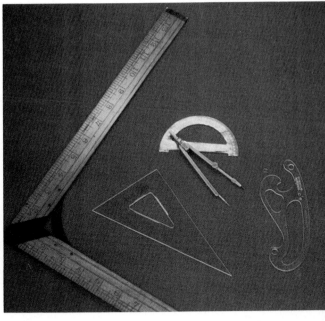

Left: Different sizes of screwdrivers. Right: Tools for making square corners, circles, and other shapes and angles

Carpenters have tools for making circles and squares. They use planes to make wood smooth. They have many different kinds of hammers, screwdrivers,

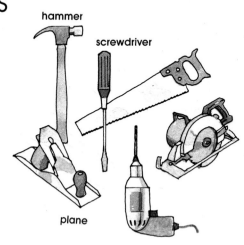

hammer

screwdriver

plane

7

Left: A power saw. Right: A measuring tape that pulls out of its case and then snaps back in

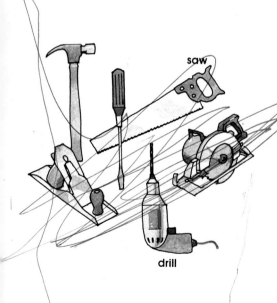

and saws. Carpenters also work with electric tools such as power saws and drills. And every carpenter has a measuring tape.

Like all other
craftspeople, carpenters
must use their heads as
well as their hands. In
high school, carpenters
study mathematics. It is
important for them to
be able to measure
things correctly.
Carpenters also study
mechanical drawing
and drafting so that
they will be able to

This construction worker (left) is studying an architect's blueprints.
Building a playhouse (right)

blueprints

read architects' blueprints and plans. Many future carpenters start working with wood when they are young. They learn how to hold a hammer properly and how to saw straight. It's fun to build tree houses and coaster cars.

The best way to become a carpenter is to start as an apprentice, or carpenter's helper. Apprentice training takes four years. Apprentice carpenters get paid while they are

Above: Drafting is one of the many subjects carpentry students study.
Below: A high school student learning carpentry in shop class

being trained on the job. They also go to classes. When their training is over, they become journeyman carpenters.

Different carpenters do different types of jobs. Rough carpenters build wooden frames for buildings. They build

Putting up partitions for the walls of a new house

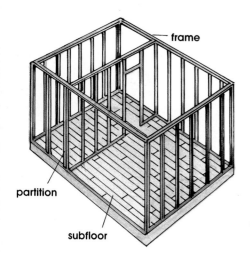

frame

partition

subfloor

partitions where walls
will be and subfloors on
which floors will be laid.
   Rough carpenters
also work on highways,
dams, and bridges.
They build the forms
into which cement is
poured.

14

Above: Building a wooden subfloor
Below: Carpenters working on a new highway

window frame

cabinet

Finish carpenters are those who hang doors in place and install window frames and cabinets. They must do their work well so that windows and doors open and close properly. Some finish carpenters lay the boards for wooden floors.

Above: Carpenters installing a window
Below: Carpenters laying a hardwood floor and finishing a cabinet

Left: Carpenters setting up an electric saw on a construction site
Right: Carpenters have many jobs to do on a high-rise building project.

Whatever they do,
finish carpenters have
to work quickly. But they
must also be sure their
finished work looks
good.

Maintenance carpenters are needed everywhere. Their job is to keep buildings and equipment in good repair. Many maintenance carpenters do both rough work and finish work.

Cabinetmakers are highly skilled and

Making furniture such as cabinets (above)
and tables (below) is a special carpentry skill.

artistic carpenters. They make cabinets and furniture. Cabinetmakers—and many finish and maintenance carpenters—do almost all their work indoors. Carpenters who work indoors can have jobs all year long, no matter what the weather is like outdoors.

Above: Ships' carpenters building a boat at Rocky Harbour, Newfoundland
Below: Repairing a boat at Boothbay Harbor, Maine

There are carpenters who build sets in movie and television studios. There are ship carpenters who do repairs at sea. Carpenters' skills will also be needed in outer space. Carpenters can take their toolboxes and go almost anywhere!

set

TV studio

toolbox

A carpenter's hands
and eyes should work
well together. And
carpenters should not
be afraid of heights.
They may have to work
on scaffolds or high
ladders.

scaffold

If you become a
carpenter, you may
work while walking,
standing, or climbing.
Carpenters seldom
sit down on the job!

Opposite page: Carpenter working on a scaffold

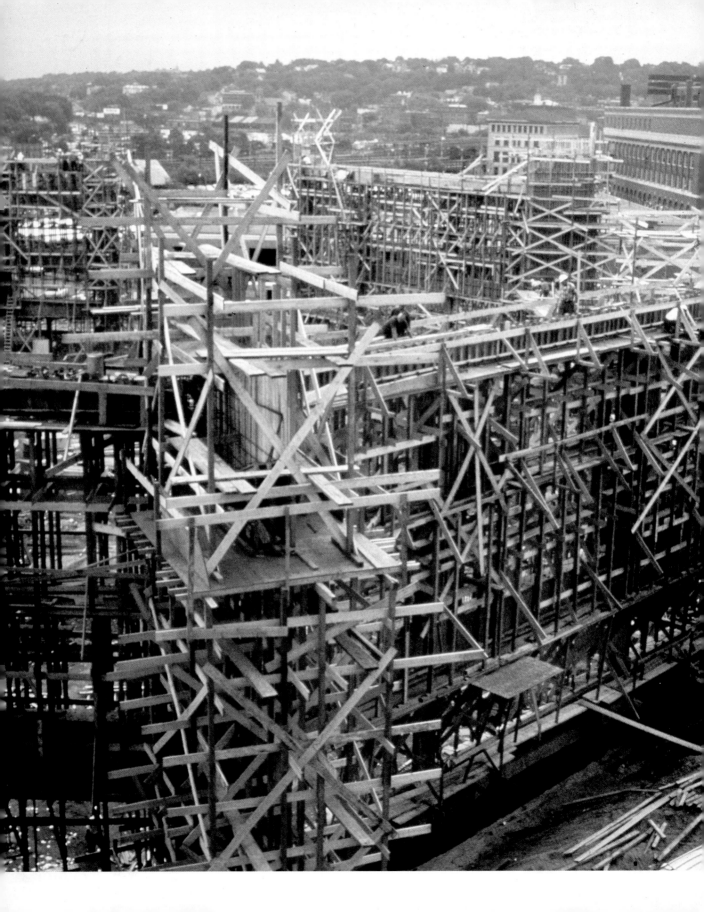

On construction sites, carpenters work with plumbers, electricians, bricklayers, and masons. A carpenter in a construction crew must get along well with others. Carpenters must also be able to work in a safe and careful manner.

Long ago, the first carpenters built huts with crude stone axes. Today, carpenters are highly skilled and use many kinds of tools. In the future, there may be new ways to build. But the world will always need carpenters. If *you* like to build things, you could be one of them.

WORDS YOU SHOULD KNOW

apprentice (uh • PREN • tiss)—someone who is being trained on the job by a skilled worker

architect (ARK • ih • tekt)—a person whose job is to draw plans for new buildings

axe (AX)—a tool with a wooden handle and a metal blade for chopping wood

blueprints (BLOO • prints)—drawings of an architect's plans for a building

bricklayer (BRIK • lay • er)—a construction worker who puts bricks into place

cement (sih • MENT)—a grey powder made of many minerals that is mixed with sand and water to make concrete

construction site (kun • STRUK • shun SITE)—location where a building or other large structure is being built

drafting—drawing plans for something to be built

drill—a tool for making small, round holes. Some drills are worked by hand and some are electric.

electrician (ih • lek • TRIH • shun)—a worker who installs and repairs electric wires

heights (HITES)—high places

install —to build something into its place

journeyman (JER • nee • mun)—someone who has learned a trade and is working for another skilled worker

maintenance (MANE • teh • nents)—repairing something or keeping it in good repair

mason (MAY • sun)—a worker who builds with stone, brick, or concrete blocks

partition (par • TEE • shun)—the supporting structure behind an indoor wall

plane—a tool with handles and a sharp blade for cutting the rough surface from wood to make it smooth

plumber (PLUM • er)—a worker who installs and repairs water pipes

power saw —an electric tool for cutting wood

saw—a tool for cutting wood

scaffold (SKAF • uld)—a platform for workers to stand on when working in high places

subfloor—the supporting structure under a floor

INDEX

PHOTO CREDITS

© Reinhard Brucker—7 (left)

Cameramann International, Ltd.—18 (right),
20 (2 photos)

Gartman Agency:
© Michael Philip Manheim—10 (right)

© Virginia Grimes—8 (left), 15 (top),
17 (bottom), 18 (left)

Image Finders:
© R. Flanagan—8 (right), 12 (bottom)

Journalism Services:
© James H. Martin—6 (left)
© John Patsch—4 (bottom)
© Rene Sheret—4 (top), 14, 15 (bottom)
© Steve Sumner—28 (bottom right)

Nawrocki Stock Photo:
© Phylane Norman—6 (center), 28 (top)

© Art Pahlke—17 (top), 24

Photori—7 (right), 10 (left), 22 (bottom), 26

R/C Photo Agency:
© Richard L. Capps—12 (top)
© Earl L. Kubis—6 (right)

Tom Stack and Associates—Cover

Courtesy U.S. Department of Labor/American
Petroleum Institute—28 (bottom left)

Valan Photos:
© Alan Wilkinson—22 (top)

ABOUT THE AUTHOR

Dee Lillegard (born Deanna Quintel) is the author of over two hundred published stories, poems, and puzzles for children—plus *Word Skills*, a series of high-interest grammar worktexts, and *September to September, Poems for All Year 'Round*, a teacher resource. Ms. Lillegard has also worked as a children's book editor and teaches writing for children in the San Francisco Bay area. She is a native Californian.